contents

British & North American Readers
Please note that Australian cup and spoon
measurements are metric. A quick conversion
guide appears on page 63.

The wok: seasoning & care

Once it has been properly seasoned, a wok is an easy-care addition to your kitchen arsenal. Read the following tips and you'll soon be ready to roll with your wok.

Wok choices

Woks are available in many sizes (ranging from 25cm to 60cm diameter) and in a huge variety of finishes – choose between cast-iron, stainless steel, forge-cast or anodised aluminium, non-stick and the traditional carbon-steel wok. Round-based woks are best suited to gas burners, while flat-based woks are the ideal match for electric and halogen stovetops; portable electric woks are also available.

Seasoning a wok

Stainless steel and non-stick woks don't require seasoning. If you choose a wok made of carbon steel or cast iron, though, you should season your wok before using it for the first time. This prepares the wok for the extremely high temperatures it has to endure – wok cooking is, after all, fast cooking at searing temperatures. Follow these step-by-step instructions to season your wok.

- First, wash the wok in hot soapy water to remove all traces of grease, then dry it thoroughly.
- Place the wok over high heat; when it is hot, use absorbent paper to rub approximately 1 tablespoon of cooking oil all over the inside surface.

- Leave the wok over high heat for about 10 minutes, wiping at times with a ball of absorbent paper.
- Repeat this process twice.

Be warned: seasoning a wok this way creates a fair amount of smoke, as you're effectively burning the oil off the surface of the wok. For your own safety, you should wear oven gloves when holding the wok and the oil-soaked absorbent paper.

Wok care tips

- After every use, wash your wok in hot, soapy water with a sponge or cloth – never use scourers, steel wool or harsh abrasives. Thoroughly dry the wok by placing it on the cook top, over low heat, for a few minutes. Rub or spray a thin layer of cooking oil all over the inside surface of the wok before storing – this will prevent rust.
- A wok chan is a shovel-like utensil used for lifting, tossing and stirring food. Traditionally made of metal, these are ideal for use in carbon-steel and cast-iron woks. Plastic wok chans are the utensil of choice for use with a non-stick wok, as they won't scratch the surface – or you could use a wooden spatula.

lamb and cashew stir-fry

2 tablespoons peanut oil
700g lamb eye of loin, sliced thinly
1 medium red capsicum (200g), sliced thinly
150g oyster mushrooms
500g spinach, trimmed
¼ cup (60ml) oyster sauce
2 tablespoons soy sauce
3 cloves garlic, crushed
1 teaspoon grated fresh ginger
1 tablespoon brown sugar
2 teaspoons cornflour
1 tablespoon water
2 tablespoons coarsely shredded fresh basil
1 cup (150g) roasted cashews

Heat half of the oil in wok; stir-fry lamb,
in batches, until browned all over and almost
cooked through. Heat remaining oil in wok; stir-fry
capsicum and mushrooms until just tender.
Return lamb to wok with spinach, sauces, garlic,
ginger, sugar and blended cornflour and water;
stir-fry until sauce boils and thickens slightly.
Serve sprinkled with basil and nuts.

serves 4
per serving 34.5g fat; 2371kJ
on the table in 30 minutes

thai chicken noodle stir-fry

180g dried rice noodles
700g chicken breast fillets, sliced thinly
2 teaspoons grated fresh ginger
2 tablespoons peanut oil
1$\frac{1}{2}$ cups (120g) bean sprouts
300g baby bok choy, chopped coarsely
$\frac{1}{3}$ cup (80ml) lime juice
$\frac{1}{4}$ cup (60ml) sweet chilli sauce
2 teaspoons fish sauce
1$\frac{1}{2}$ tablespoons caster sugar
2 tablespoons chopped fresh coriander
$\frac{1}{3}$ cup torn fresh mint leaves
4 green onions, sliced thinly

Place noodles in large heatproof bowl; cover with
boiling water. Stand 5 minutes or until tender; drain.
Meanwhile, combine chicken and ginger in
medium bowl. Heat oil in wok; stir-fry chicken
mixture, in batches, until cooked through.
Return chicken to wok with sprouts, bok choy
and combined juice, sauces, sugar, coriander
and mint; stir until hot. Add onion and noodles;
stir-fry until hot.

serves 4
per serving 20g fat; 2162kJ
on the table in 30 minutes

beef with oyster sauce and mushrooms

2 tablespoons peanut oil
600g beef rump steak, sliced thinly
1 medium red capsicum (200g), sliced thinly
350g broccoli, cut into florets
2 cloves garlic, crushed
2 teaspoons cornflour
1/4 cup (60ml) water
1 tablespoon soy sauce
1/4 cup (60ml) oyster sauce
1 teaspoon sesame oil
2 tablespoons rice wine vinegar
150g snow peas, halved lengthways
150g oyster mushrooms

Heat half of the peanut oil in wok; stir-fry beef, in batches, until browned all over.
Heat remaining peanut oil in wok; stir-fry capsicum, broccoli and garlic until vegetables are just tender.
Add combined cornflour, water, sauces, sesame oil and rice wine vinegar to wok; bring to a boil.
Return beef to wok, add snow peas and mushrooms; stir-fry until heated through.
Serve with steamed rice, if desired.

serves 4
per serving 25.3g fat; 1663kJ
on the table in 20 minutes

lemon veal stir-fry with capsicum and pecans

1 tablespoon peanut oil
600g veal steaks, sliced thinly
2 medium brown onions (300g), cut into thin wedges
1 medium red capsicum (200g), sliced thinly
1 medium green capsicum (200g), sliced thinly
2 tablespoons finely chopped fresh lemon grass
1/3 cup (35g) pecans, halved lengthways
2 teaspoons grated lemon rind
1/3 cup (80ml) lemon juice
1/3 cup (80ml) soy sauce
1 clove garlic, crushed

Heat oil in wok; stir-fry veal, in batches,
until browned.
Add onion, capsicums and lemon grass
to wok; stir-fry until vegetables are soft.
Stir in nuts; cook 1 minute.
Return veal to wok with combined rind, juice,
sauce and garlic; stir-fry until heated through.

serves 4
per serving 14.7g fat; 1311kJ
on the table in 30 minutes

pork with chinese cabbage and noodles

375g fresh egg noodles
1 tablespoon peanut oil
1 clove garlic, crushed
2 teaspoons finely chopped fresh lemon grass
1/2 teaspoon five-spice powder
400g pork fillets, sliced thinly
1 medium red capsicum (200g), sliced thinly
5 green onions, chopped coarsely
1/4 medium chinese cabbage (200g),
   shredded coarsely
2 tablespoons oyster sauce
1 tablespoon soy sauce
2 tablespoons mild sweet chilli sauce
2 teaspoons sesame oil
1/2 teaspoon cornflour
2/3 cup (160ml) chicken stock

Cook noodles in large saucepan of boiling water, uncovered, until just tender; drain.

Meanwhile, heat half of the peanut oil in wok; stir-fry garlic, lemon grass and five-spice until fragrant. Add pork; stir-fry until pork is browned and cooked through, remove from wok.

Heat remaining peanut oil in wok; stir-fry capsicum, onion and cabbage until cabbage is just wilted.

Return pork to wok, add sauces, sesame oil and blended cornflour and stock; stir until mixture boils and thickens slightly. Serve pork on noodles.

serves 4
per serving 11g fat; 1930kJ
on the table in 35 minutes

pad thai

12 medium cooked prawns (300g)
250g dried rice noodles
2 tablespoons brown sugar
1 tablespoon lime juice
1 tablespoon soy sauce
1 tablespoon tomato sauce
2 tablespoons mild chilli sauce
2 tablespoons fish sauce
2 teaspoons peanut oil
200g chicken mince
200g pork mince
1 clove garlic, crushed
1 tablespoon grated fresh ginger
3 eggs, beaten lightly
2 green onions, sliced thinly
1 cup (80g) bean sprouts
1/2 cup (75g) roasted unsalted peanuts,
   chopped coarsely
1/3 cup chopped fresh coriander

Shell and devein prawns, leaving tails intact.
Place noodles in large heatproof bowl; cover with
boiling water. Stand until just tender; drain.
Meanwhile, combine sugar, juice and sauces in
small bowl. Heat oil in wok; stir-fry chicken, pork,
garlic and ginger until meat is cooked through.
Add prawns and egg to wok; gently stir-fry until
egg sets. Add noodles, sauce mixture and
remaining ingredients; stir-fry gently until hot.

serves 4
per serving 24g fat; 2535kJ
on the table in 30 minutes

hokkien mee noodles

Kecap manis, a sweet, thick, Indonesian soy sauce, is available from all Asian grocery stores and most large supermarkets.

600g hokkien noodles
2 tablespoons vegetable oil
2 cloves garlic, crushed
2 teaspoons grated fresh ginger
3 kaffir lime leaves, chopped finely
1 large red capsicum (350g), sliced thinly
500g baby bok choy, chopped coarsely
6 green onions, chopped coarsely
1 cup (80g) bean sprouts
1 teaspoon cornflour
1/3 cup (80ml) kecap manis
2 tablespoons sweet chilli sauce
1 teaspoon sesame oil
1 tablespoon water

Place noodles in large heatproof bowl; cover with boiling water, separate with fork, drain.
Meanwhile, heat vegetable oil in wok; stir-fry garlic, ginger, lime leaves, capsicum and bok choy until vegetables are almost tender.
Add onion, sprouts and noodles; stir to combine. Blend cornflour with kecap manis, sauce, sesame oil and the water, add to wok; stir-fry until mixture boils and thickens slightly.

serves 4
per serving 11.6g fat; 1390kJ
on the table in 20 minutes

mongolian garlic lamb

700g lamb fillets, sliced thinly
3 cloves garlic, crushed
1/4 cup (60ml) soy sauce
1/3 cup (80ml) sweet sherry
1 tablespoon cornflour
2 tablespoons vegetable oil
1 tablespoon brown sugar
1 teaspoon sesame oil
8 green onions, sliced thinly

Combine lamb, garlic, half of the sauce, half of the sherry and cornflour in large bowl; mix well.
Heat vegetable oil in wok; stir-fry lamb mixture, in batches, until browned all over.
Return lamb mixture to wok. Add remaining sauce, remaining sherry, sugar and sesame oil; stir-fry until sauce boils and thickens slightly. Remove from heat; stir in onion.
Serve on a bed of stir-fried baby bok choy and steamed rice, if desired.

serves 4
per serving 16.8g fat; 1486kJ
on the table in 20 minutes

fried noodles, chicken and bok choy

250g dried rice noodles
1 tablespoon peanut oil
3 eggs, beaten lightly
1 medium brown onion (150g), chopped finely
2 cloves garlic, crushed
2 teaspoons grated fresh ginger
500g chicken mince
500g baby bok choy, chopped coarsely
1/4 cup (60ml) soy sauce
1/2 cup chopped fresh coriander
3 cups (240g) bean sprouts

Place noodles in large heatproof bowl; cover with boiling water. Stand 5 minutes or until just tender; drain.

Meanwhile, brush heated wok with a little of the oil. Add half of the egg, swirl to cover base of wok; cook until set. Remove omelette from wok; repeat with remaining egg. Roll omelettes tightly; slice thinly.

Heat remaining oil in wok; stir-fry onion, garlic and ginger until onion softens. Add chicken; stir-fry until chicken is cooked through. Add bok choy, sauce and coriander; stir-fry until bok choy is just tender. Stir in noodles and sprouts; serve topped with omelette.

serves 4
per serving 19.8g fat; 2149kJ
on the table in 30 minutes

spicy beef fillet with bean sprouts

700g piece beef fillet
1 teaspoon soy sauce
1 teaspoon sesame oil
1 teaspoon cornflour
1 tablespoon water
1½ tablespoons peanut oil
2 medium brown onions (300g), sliced thinly
1 clove garlic, crushed
1 teaspoon mild curry powder
1 tablespoon satay sauce
2 teaspoons soy sauce, extra
1 teaspoon brown sugar
2 teaspoons dry sherry
2 tablespoons water, extra
1 cup (80g) bean sprouts

Cut beef into 5mm-thick slices, flatten slightly with meat mallet. Combine beef in medium bowl with soy sauce, sesame oil, cornflour and the water; stand 10 minutes.

Heat 1 tablespoon of the peanut oil in wok; stir-fry beef, in batches, until browned both sides.

Heat remaining peanut oil in wok; stir-fry onion, garlic and curry powder until fragrant. Add satay sauce, extra soy sauce, sugar, sherry and extra water; bring to a boil.

Return beef to wok; stir-fry until heated through. Toss in bean sprouts.

serves 4
per serving 17.8g fat; 1471kJ
on the table in 40 minutes

stir-fried pork and vegetables

1 tablespoon peanut oil
500g pork fillet, sliced thinly
1 medium red onion (170g), sliced thickly
600g bok choy, halved lengthways
300g baby green beans
400g fresh asparagus, halved
2 tablespoons black bean sauce
$3/4$ cup (180ml) water
2 tablespoons honey
$1/3$ cup (80ml) soy sauce
2 teaspoons grated fresh ginger
1 tablespoon cornflour

Heat half of the oil in wok; stir-fry pork, in batches, until browned and cooked through.
Heat remaining oil in wok; stir-fry onion until soft. Add bok choy, beans and asparagus; stir-fry until vegetables are tender. Stir in combined remaining ingredients.
Return pork to wok. Stir-fry until mixture boils and thickens.

serves 4
per serving 8.3g fat; 1294kJ
on the table in 30 minutes

stir-fried seafood with asian greens

20 medium uncooked prawns (500g)
500g squid hoods
500g firm white fish fillets
1 tablespoon peanut oil
5 green onions, chopped coarsely
2 cloves garlic, sliced thinly
50g fresh ginger, peeled, sliced thinly
500g baby bok choy, chopped coarsely
500g choy sum, chopped coarsely
2 tablespoons soy sauce
2 tablespoons oyster sauce
1 tablespoon mild chilli sauce

Shell and devein prawns, leaving tails intact.
Cut squid hoods in half. Score inside surface of
each piece; cut into 5cm-wide strips. Cut fish
into 3cm pieces.
Heat half of the oil in wok; stir-fry seafood,
in batches, until lightly browned all over and
cooked through. Heat remaining oil in wok;
stir-fry onion, garlic and ginger until onion softens.
Return seafood to wok. Add bok choy,
choy sum and combined sauces; stir-fry until
greens are just wilted and heated through.

serves 4
per serving 9.8g fat; 1524kJ
on the table in 40 minutes

stir-fried vegetables with rice noodles

250g dried rice noodles
1 tablespoon peanut oil
1 teaspoon sesame oil
1 large brown onion (200g), sliced thickly
1 clove garlic, crushed
$1/4$ cup (60ml) soy sauce
$1/3$ cup (80ml) sweet chilli sauce
2 teaspoons cornflour
$1/2$ cup (125ml) water
2 teaspoons grated fresh ginger
1 tablespoon sweet sherry
1 medium red capsicum (200g), chopped coarsely
180g broccoli florets
150g snow peas, halved lengthways
425g can baby corn cuts, drained,
    halved lengthways

Place noodles in medium heatproof bowl, cover with boiling water, stand until tender; drain.
Meanwhile, heat oils in wok; stir-fry onion and garlic until onion softens. Add combined sauces, blended cornflour and water, ginger and sherry; stir until sauce boils and slightly thickens.
Add capsicum, broccoli, snow peas and corn; stir-fry until vegetables are just tender.
Serve noodles with stir-fried vegetables.

serves 4
per serving 8g fat; 1601kJ
on the table in 25 minutes

balinese-style lamb

Kecap manis, a sweet, thick, Indonesian soy sauce, is available from all Asian grocery stores and most large supermarkets. You will need a piece of ginger about 5cm long for this recipe.

5 fresh red thai chillies, seeded, chopped coarsely
2 teaspoons fish sauce
2 medium brown onions (300g), chopped coarsely
3 cloves garlic, quartered
50g fresh ginger, peeled, chopped coarsely
2 tablespoons desiccated coconut, toasted
1 tablespoon peanut oil
700g lamb fillets, sliced thinly
1 tablespoon brown sugar
1 tablespoon kecap manis
1 tablespoon soy sauce
1 tablespoon lime juice

Blend or process chilli, sauce, onion, garlic, ginger and coconut until mixture forms a paste.
Heat oil in wok; stir-fry lamb, in batches, until browned all over. Add chilli mixture to wok; stir-fry until fragrant.
Return lamb to wok with combined remaining ingredients; stir-fry until heated through.
Serve with steamed jasmine rice and stir-fried sugar snap peas, if desired.

serves 4
per serving 13g fat; 1288kJ
on the table in 30 minutes

quick & easy side dishes

There's no limit to the delicious food that can come to life in your wok.
These stylish side dishes will lend any meal a little class.

asian greens in oyster sauce

1 cup (250ml) chicken stock
⅓ cup (80ml) oyster sauce
2 teaspoons sesame oil
2kg baby bok choy, trimmed
1kg choy sum, trimmed

Combine stock, sauce and oil in wok;
bring mixture to a boil. Add bok choy;
cook, stirring, about 3 minutes or until
bok choy is slightly wilted.
Stir in choy sum; cook, covered,
about 5 minutes or until both greens
are tender and just wilted.

serves 6
per serving 2.5g fat; 264kJ
on the table in 15 minutes

beans and sugar snap peas with lemon and capers

300g butter beans
200g sugar snap peas
2 teaspoons olive oil
2 tablespoons drained tiny capers
¼ cup (60ml) lemon juice
2 tablespoons chopped fresh dill

Boil, steam or microwave beans and
peas, separately, until just tender; drain.
Heat oil in wok; cook capers, stirring,
until browned lightly.
Add juice, beans and peas; stir-fry
until vegetables are hot. Stir in dill.

serves 4
per serving 2.6g fat; 244kJ
on the table in 20 minutes

asparagus with citrus-toasted breadcrumbs

40g butter
2 tablespoons peanut oil
1½ cups (105g) stale breadcrumbs
2 tablespoons finely grated orange rind
2 cloves garlic, crushed
750g fresh asparagus, trimmed
8 sprigs fresh tarragon
1 cup (80g) flaked parmesan

Heat half of the butter and half of the oil in wok; stir-fry combined breadcrumbs and rind until lightly browned, remove from wok.
Heat remaining butter and oil in wok; stir-fry garlic and asparagus, in batches, until asparagus is tender.
Serve asparagus sprinkled with tarragon, breadcrumbs and cheese.

serves 6
per serving 16.6g fat; 1017kJ
on the table in 20 minutes

spinach with toasted almonds

2 teaspoons peanut oil
2 tablespoons rice wine vinegar
2 tablespoons soy sauce
2 tablespoons honey
1 clove garlic, crushed
1 teaspoon grated fresh ginger
1kg spinach
4 green onions, chopped coarsely
½ cup (40g) flaked almonds, toasted

Heat oil in wok, add vinegar, sauce, honey, garlic and ginger; bring to a boil.
Add spinach and onion; stir-fry until spinach is just wilted.
Serve sprinkled with nuts.

serves 4
per serving 8.2g fat; 639kJ
on the table in 15 minutes

chicken satay noodles

2 teaspoons ground coriander
2 teaspoons ground cumin
2 teaspoons ground turmeric
700g chicken thigh fillets, chopped coarsely
250g hokkien noodles
6 green onions
150g fresh baby corn
2 tablespoons peanut oil
1 large carrot (180g), sliced thinly
2 tablespoons chopped fresh coriander

satay sauce
1/2 cup (130g) crunchy peanut butter
1/2 cup (125ml) coconut cream
1/2 cup (125ml) chicken stock
2 tablespoons sweet chilli sauce
2 tablespoons soy sauce
1 tablespoon brown sugar
1 tablespoon lime juice

Combine spices in medium bowl, add chicken; mix well to coat with spices.

Place noodles in large heatproof bowl; cover with boiling water, separate with fork, drain.

Chop onions and corn diagonally into 4cm pieces.

Heat half of the oil in wok; stir-fry chicken, in batches, until browned. Heat remaining oil in wok; stir-fry corn and carrot until just tender.

Return chicken to wok with noodles, onion, satay sauce and coriander; stir-fry until heated through.

Satay sauce Combine ingredients in medium jug; whisk until well combined.

serves 4
per serving 46g fat; 3107kJ
on the table in 25 minutes

teriyaki beef

1/2 cup (125ml) mirin
1/3 cup (80ml) light soy sauce
1/4 cup (50g) firmly packed brown sugar
1 tablespoon grated fresh ginger
1 clove garlic, crushed
1 teaspoon sesame oil
1 tablespoon sesame seeds
700g beef fillet, sliced thinly
300g fresh baby corn, halved
2 green onions, sliced thinly

Combine mirin, sauce, sugar, ginger, garlic, oil and seeds in large bowl. Stir in beef and corn; stand 5 minutes.

Drain beef mixture over medium saucepan; reserve marinade in pan. Cook beef and corn, in batches, in heated wok until browned all over and cooked as desired.

Meanwhile, bring marinade to a boil. Reduce heat; simmer, uncovered, 5 minutes.

Serve beef and corn drizzled with hot marinade; sprinkle with onion.

serves 4
per serving 12g fat; 1730kJ
on the table in 30 minutes

fried rice

Kecap manis, a sweet, thick, Indonesian soy sauce, is available from all Asian grocery stores and most large supermarkets. You need to cook 1 cup (200g) long-grain white rice for this recipe.

1 tablespoon peanut oil
2 eggs, beaten lightly
120g baby corn, halved
1 trimmed celery stick (75g), chopped finely
1 small red capsicum (150g), chopped finely
2 cloves garlic, crushed
140g ham, chopped coarsely
3 cups cooked long-grain white rice
1 tablespoon kecap manis
4 green onions, sliced thinly

Heat half of the oil in wok. Add egg, swirl to cover base of wok; cook until set. Remove omelette from wok, roll tightly; cut omelette into thin slices.
Heat remaining oil in wok; stir-fry corn and celery 2 minutes. Add capsicum, garlic and ham; stir-fry 2 minutes.
Add rice and kecap manis; stir-fry until heated through. Stir in onion and omelette.

serves 4
per serving 10g fat; 1443kJ
on the table in 20 minutes

char kway teow

1kg fresh rice noodles
500g small uncooked prawns
2 tablespoons peanut oil
340g chicken breast fillets, chopped coarsely
4 fresh red thai chillies, seeded, chopped finely
2 cloves garlic, crushed
2 teaspoons grated fresh ginger
5 green onions, sliced thinly
2 cups (160g) bean sprouts
$1/3$ cup (80ml) soy sauce
$1/4$ teaspoon sesame oil
1 teaspoon brown sugar

Place noodles in large heatproof bowl; cover with boiling water, separate with fork, drain.
Shell and devein prawns, leaving tails intact; halve prawns crossways.
Heat half of the peanut oil in wok; stir-fry chicken, chilli, garlic and ginger until chicken is cooked through. Remove from wok.
Heat remaining peanut oil in wok; stir-fry prawns until they just change colour. Remove from wok.
Stir-fry onion and sprouts in wok until onion is soft. Add noodles and combined remaining ingredients; stir-fry 1 minute.
Return chicken mixture and prawns to wok; stir-fry until heated through.

serves 6
per serving 10.4g fat; 1464kJ
on the table in 40 minutes

hot and sweet mixed vegetables

500g chinese broccoli
1 tablespoon peanut oil
2 cloves garlic, crushed
1 tablespoon grated fresh ginger
300g tat soi, trimmed
300g baby bok choy, chopped coarsely
300g chinese cabbage, chopped coarsely
2 tablespoons soy sauce
$\frac{1}{4}$ cup (60ml) chinese barbecue sauce
2 tablespoons sweet chilli sauce
$1\frac{1}{2}$ cups (120g) bean sprouts

Discard tough ends from broccoli; chop broccoli coarsely.
Heat oil in wok; stir-fry garlic and ginger until fragrant. Add broccoli, tat soi, bok choy, cabbage and combined sauces; stir-fry until vegetables are just tender. Remove wok from heat; stir in bean sprouts.

serves 4
per serving 5.5g fat; 528kJ
on the table in 15 minutes

honey chilli chicken

vegetable oil, for deep-frying
100g bean thread vermicelli
1 tablespoon peanut oil
2 medium brown onions (300g), sliced thinly
4 cloves garlic, crushed
1 tablespoon grated fresh ginger
700g chicken thigh fillets, halved
½ cup (175g) honey
2 tablespoons sweet chilli sauce
500g chinese broccoli, chopped coarsely
¼ cup coarsely chopped fresh garlic chives

Heat vegetable oil in wok; deep-fry noodles, in batches, until puffed and white. Drain noodles on absorbent paper.

Heat peanut oil in wok; stir-fry onion, garlic and ginger until fragrant. Add chicken, honey and sauce; stir-fry until chicken is browned and cooked through.

Add broccoli and chives; stir-fry until broccoli is just tender. Serve over noodles.

serves 4
per serving 22.3g fat; 2445kJ
on the table in 40 minutes

beef coconut curry

2 tablespoons peanut oil
500g beef rump steak, sliced thinly
1 medium brown onion (150g), sliced thinly
2 teaspoons grated fresh ginger
1 clove garlic, crushed
1/3 cup (100g) mild curry paste
1 2/3 cups (400ml) coconut milk
1 medium yellow capsicum (200g), sliced thinly
150g green beans, halved

Heat half of the oil in wok; stir-fry beef,
in batches, until browned.
Heat remaining oil in wok, stir-fry onion until soft.
Add ginger, garlic and paste; stir-fry until fragrant.
Stir in coconut milk; bring to a boil.
Return beef to wok with remaining ingredients;
stir-fry until vegetables are tender.

serves 4
per serving 44.2g fat; 2355kJ
on the table in 20 minutes

sang choy bow

1 tablespoon peanut oil
700g pork mince
2 cloves garlic, crushed
225g can water chestnuts, drained, chopped finely
1 teaspoon sambal oelek
1 tablespoon lime juice
1 medium red capsicum (200g), chopped finely
1 trimmed stick celery (75g), chopped finely
2 tablespoons soy sauce
2 tablespoons rice vinegar
100g packet fried crunchy noodles
8 large iceberg lettuce leaves
2 green onions, sliced thinly

Heat oil in wok; stir-fry pork and garlic until pork is cooked through.

Stir in water chestnuts, sambal, juice, capsicum, celery, sauce and vinegar; cook, stirring, until vegetables are just tender.

Remove from heat; stir in noodles. Divide pork mixture among lettuce leaves; sprinkle with onion.

serves 4
per serving 20.5g fat; 1620kJ
on the table in 30 minutes

mustard-seed chilli prawns

20 large uncooked prawns (1kg)
1/4 teaspoon ground turmeric
2 fresh red thai chillies, seeded, chopped finely
2 tablespoons vegetable oil
2 teaspoons black mustard seeds
2 cloves garlic, crushed
2 tablespoons chopped fresh coriander

Shell and devein prawns, leaving tails intact.
Cut along back of prawn, taking care not to cut
all the way through; flatten prawn slightly.
Wearing disposable gloves, rub turmeric and
chilli into prawns in medium bowl.
Heat oil in wok; cook mustard seeds and garlic,
stirring, until seeds start to pop. Add prawn
mixture; stir-fry until prawns just change colour.
Stir in coriander.

serves 4
per serving 10.1g fat; 823kJ
on the table in 30 minutes

chinese cabbage and tofu stir-fry

You will need one small chinese cabbage to make this recipe.

250g dried rice noodles
2 tablespoons peanut oil
300g firm tofu, chopped coarsely
1 clove garlic, crushed
1 fresh red thai chilli, sliced thinly
200g button mushrooms, quartered
1/3 cup (80ml) black bean sauce
1/3 cup (80ml) vegetable stock
300g finely shredded chinese cabbage
1 cup (80g) bean sprouts
3 green onions, sliced thinly
2 tablespoons chopped fresh coriander

Place noodles in medium heatproof bowl, cover with boiling water, stand until tender; drain.

Meanwhile, heat half of the oil in wok; stir-fry tofu until browned all over. Drain on absorbent paper.

Heat remaining oil in wok; stir-fry garlic, chilli and mushrooms until tender. Stir in sauce and stock; bring to a boil. Add cabbage; stir-fry until just wilted.

Remove from heat; stir in tofu, sprouts, onion and coriander. Serve noodles topped with chinese cabbage and tofu stir-fry.

serves 4
per serving 16g fat; 1699kJ
on the table in 25 minutes

chicken and almond stir-fry

2 tablespoons peanut oil
1 cup (160g) blanched whole almonds
600g chicken tenderloins
1 teaspoon grated fresh ginger
2 tablespoons hoisin sauce
1 small leek (200g), sliced thickly
200g green beans, halved
2 green onions, chopped finely
1 tablespoon soy sauce
1 tablespoon plum sauce
1 teaspoon sesame oil

Heat half of the peanut oil in wok; stir-fry almonds until browned, remove from wok.
Stir-fry chicken in wok, in batches, until browned and just cooked through.
Heat remaining peanut oil in wok, add ginger; stir-fry until fragrant. Add hoisin sauce, leek and beans; stir-fry until beans are just tender.
Return chicken to wok with onion, soy sauce, plum sauce and sesame oil; stir-fry until heated through. Toss through almonds.

serves 4
per serving 41.5g fat; 2466kJ
on the table in 25 minutes

spicy pork spare ribs

1.5kg pork spare ribs, chopped
1 tablespoon peanut oil
$^1/_4$ cup (60ml) chinese barbecue sauce
2 tablespoons soy sauce
2 tablespoons sweet chilli sauce
2 cloves garlic, crushed
2 teaspoons grated fresh ginger
$^1/_4$ cup (90g) honey
$^1/_3$ cup (75g) firmly packed brown sugar
$^1/_4$ teaspoon five-spice powder
$^1/_4$ cup (60ml) dry sherry

Cook spare ribs in large saucepan of boiling water,
uncovered, about 10 minutes or until just cooked;
drain, pat dry on absorbent paper.
Heat oil in wok; stir-fry spare ribs, in batches,
until browned all over and cooked through.
Drain spare ribs on absorbent paper.
Drain oil from wok. Add remaining ingredients
to wok; bring to a boil. Add spare ribs; stir-fry
about 10 minutes, tossing until pork is well coated
in thickened sauce.

serves 4
per serving 23g fat; 2168kJ
on the table in 40 minutes

cauliflower, pea and fried tofu curry

You will need a small cauliflower weighing approximately 1kg to make this recipe.

2 tablespoons peanut oil
1 medium brown onion (150g), chopped coarsely
2 cloves garlic, crushed
900g cauliflower florets
1 teaspoon ground cumin
$1/2$ teaspoon ground coriander
$1/2$ teaspoon ground turmeric
$1/4$ teaspoon ground cayenne pepper
1 teaspoon garam masala
400g can tomatoes
1 cup (250ml) vegetable stock
400g firm tofu
$1/4$ cup (60ml) vegetable oil
1 cup (125g) frozen peas, thawed

Heat peanut oil in wok; stir-fry onion and garlic until onion softens. Add cauliflower and spices; cook, stirring, 2 minutes.

Add undrained crushed tomatoes and stock, stir to combine; bring to a boil. Reduce heat; simmer, covered, 10 minutes or until cauliflower softens slightly.

Meanwhile, cut tofu into 1cm cubes. Heat vegetable oil in medium frying pan; cook tofu, in batches, until lightly coloured and crisp on all sides, drain on absorbent paper. Add tofu and peas to cauliflower curry.

serves 4
per serving 22.2g fat; 1436kJ
on the table in 40 minutes

glossary

bean sprouts also known as bean shoots.

black bean sauce made from fermented soy beans, spices, water and flour.

black mustard seeds also known as brown mustard seeds; more pungent than the white (or yellow) seeds.

bok choy also known as bak choy, pak choi, chinese white cabbage and chinese chard. Has a mild mustard taste; both stems and leaves are used. Baby bok choy is smaller and more tender than bok choy.

breadcrumbs, stale one-or two-day-old bread made into crumbs by grating, blending or processing.

butter use salted or unsalted (sweet) butter; 125g is equal to one stick of butter.

butter beans also called wax or yellow beans, they are a variety of green or french bean, cooked and eaten in similar ways.

capers the grey-green buds of a warm-climate shrub; sold either dried and salted or pickled in vinegar brine.

capsicum also known as bell pepper or, simply, pepper. They can be red, green, yellow, orange or purplish black. Seeds and membranes should be discarded before use.

cayenne pepper thin-fleshed, long, extremely hot red chilli; usually purchased dried and ground.

chilli, thai small, hot chilli, bright-red to dark-green in colour.

chinese barbecue sauce a thick, sweet and salty commercial sauce; made from fermented soy beans, vinegar, garlic, pepper and spices. Available from Asian food stores.

chinese broccoli also known as gai lum, gai larn and chinese kale.

chinese cabbage also known as peking or napa cabbage, wong bok and petsai; this elongated cabbage has pale-green crinkly leaves.

choy sum also known as flowering bok choy, flowering white cabbage or chinese flowering cabbage. The stems, leaves and yellow flowers are served steamed, stir-fried and in soups.

coconut cream the first pressing from grated, mature coconut flesh; available in cans and cartons.

coconut milk the second pressing (less rich) from grated mature coconut flesh; available in cans and cartons, and in a reduced-fat form.

cornflour also known as cornstarch; used as a thickening agent in cooking.

fish sauce also called nam pla or nuoc nam; made from pulverised salted fermented fish. Has a pungent smell and strong taste; use sparingly.

five-spice powder a fragrant blend of ground cinnamon, clove, star anise, sichuan pepper and fennel seeds.

hoisin sauce a thick, sweet and spicy Chinese paste made from salted, fermented soy beans, onions and garlic.

kaffir lime leaves aromatic leaves of a small citrus tree bearing a wrinkled-skinned yellow-green fruit.

kecap manis Indonesian thick soy sauce which has sugar and spices added.

lemon grass a tall, clumping, lemon-smelling and -tasting, sharp-edged grass; the white lower part of each stem is used in cooking.

mince also known as ground meat, as in beef, chicken, pork, lamb and veal.

mirin a Japanese champagne-coloured cooking wine made of glutinous rice and alcohol; do not confuse with sake.

mushrooms
button: small, cultivated white mushrooms with mild flavour.
oyster: also known as abalone mushrooms or shellfish of the woods, these mushrooms have a fan-shaped fluted cap and range in colour from pearly-white to peach or grey.

noodles
bean thread vermicelli: also known as bean thread noodles, or cellophane or glass noodles. Made from green mung bean flour.
dried rice: dried noodle made from rice flour and water; available flat and wide or thin.
fresh egg: made from wheat flour and eggs; strands vary in thickness.
fresh rice: soft white noodles made from rice flour and oil; available in varying thicknesses from vermicelli-thin to broad and flat. Rinse under hot water before using, to remove starch and excess oil.

hokkien: also known as stir-fry noodles; fresh wheat flour noodles resembling thick, yellow-brown spaghetti.

packaged fried crunchy: already deep-fried; sometimes labelled crunchy noodles.

oil

peanut: made from ground peanuts; most commonly used oil in Asian cooking due to its high smoke point.

sesame: made from roasted, crushed white sesame seeds; used as a flavouring, not a cooking medium.

onion

green: also known as scallion or (incorrectly) shallot; an immature onion picked before the bulb has formed, having a long, bright-green edible stalk.

red: also known as spanish, red spanish or bermuda onion; a sweet-flavoured, large, purple-red onion.

oyster sauce Asian in origin, this rich, brown sauce is made from oysters and their brine, cooked with salt and soy sauce, and thickened with starches.

paprika ground dried red capsicum (bell pepper), available sweet or hot.

plum sauce a thick, sweet and sour sauce made from plums, vinegar, sugar, chillies and spices.

prawns also known as shrimp.

rice vinegar a colourless vinegar made from fermented rice and flavoured with sugar and salt. Also known as seasoned rice vinegar.

rice wine vinegar made from rice wine lees, salt and alcohol.

sambal oelek (also ulek or olek) Indonesian in origin; a salty paste made from ground chillies.

satay sauce traditional Indonesian/Malaysian spicy peanut sauce served with grilled meat skewers. Make your own or buy one of the many packaged versions easily obtained from supermarkets or specialty Asian food stores.

snow peas also called mange tout ("eat all"). Snow pea tendrils, the growing shoots of the plant, are sold by greengrocers.

soy sauce made from fermented soy beans. Several variations are available in most supermarkets and Asian food stores.

spinach also known as english spinach and, incorrectly, silverbeet.

squid hoods convenient cleaned squid (calamari).

stock 1 cup (250ml) stock is the equivalent of 1 cup (250ml) water plus 1 crumbled stock cube or 1 teaspoon stock powder.

sugar

brown: soft, finely granulated sugar retaining molasses for its characteristic colour and flavour.

caster: also known as superfine or finely granulated table sugar.

sugar snap peas also known as honey snap peas; snow peas can be substituted.

sweet chilli sauce a fairly mild, Thai-style sauce made from red chillies, sugar, garlic and vinegar.

tat soi also known as rosette bok choy and chinese flat cabbage; variety of bok choy developed to grow close to the ground so it is easily protected from frost.

tofu also known as bean curd; an off-white, custard-like product made from the "milk" of crushed soy beans. It is available fresh, in soft or firm varieties.

turmeric a member of the ginger family, its root is dried and ground, resulting in the rich yellow powder that gives many Indian dishes their characteristic colour. It is intensely pungent in taste but not hot.

water chestnuts small brown tubers with a crisp, white, nutty-tasting flesh. Their crunchy texture is best experienced fresh, however, canned water chestnuts are more easily obtained and can be kept about a month, once opened, under refrigeration.

zucchini also known as courgette.

index

facts & figures

These conversions are approximate only, but the difference between an exact and the approximate conversion of various liquid and dry measures is minimal and will not affect your cooking results.

Note: NZ, Canada, USA and UK all use 15ml tablespoons. Australian tablespoons measure 20ml. All cup and spoon measurements are level.

Measuring equipment

The difference between one country's measuring cups and another's is, at most, within a 2 or 3 teaspoon variance. (For the record, 1 Australian metric measuring cup holds approximately 250ml.) The most accurate way of measuring dry ingredients is to weigh them.
For liquids, use a clear glass or plastic jug having metric markings.

How to measure

When using graduated measuring cups, shake dry ingredients loosely into the appropriate cup. Do not tap the cup on a bench or tightly pack the ingredients unless directed to do so. Level the top of measuring cups and measuring spoons with a knife. When measuring liquids, place a clear glass or plastic jug having metric markings on a flat surface to check accuracy at eye level.

Dry Measures

metric	imperial
15g	1/2oz
30g	1oz
60g	2oz
90g	3oz
125g	4oz (¼lb)
155g	5oz
185g	6oz
220g	7oz
250g	8oz (½lb)
280g	9oz
315g	10oz
345g	11oz
375g	12oz (¾lb)
410g	13oz
440g	14oz
470g	15oz
500g	16oz (1lb)
750g	24oz (1½lb)
1kg	32oz (2lb)

We use large eggs having an average weight of 60g.

Liquid Measures

metric	imperial
30 ml	1 fluid oz
60 ml	2 fluid oz
100 ml	3 fluid oz
125 ml	4 fluid oz
150 ml	5 fluid oz (¼ pint/1 gill)
190 ml	6 fluid oz
250 ml (1cup)	8 fluid oz
300 ml	10 fluid oz (½ pint)
500 ml	16 fluid oz
600 ml	20 fluid oz (1 pint)
1000 ml (1litre)	1¾ pints

Helpful Measures

metric	imperial
3mm	⅛in
6mm	¼in
1cm	½in
2cm	¾in
2.5cm	1in
6cm	2½in
8cm	3in
20cm	8in
23cm	9in
25cm	10in
30cm	12in (1ft)

Oven Temperatures

These oven temperatures are only a guide.
Always check the manufacturer's manual.

	°C (Celsius)	°F (Fahrenheit)	Gas Mark
Very slow	120	250	1
Slow	150	300	2
Moderately slow	160	325	3
Moderate	180 –190	350 – 375	4
Moderately hot	200 – 210	400 – 425	5
Hot	220 – 230	450 – 475	6
Very hot	240 – 250	500 – 525	7

at your fingertips

These elegant slipcovers store up to 10 mini books and make the books instantly accessible.

And the metric measuring cups and spoons make following our recipes a piece of cake.

Book Holder
Australia and overseas:
$8.95 (incl. GST).

Metric Measuring Set
Australia: $6.50 (incl. GST).
New Zealand: $A8.00.
Elsewhere: $A9.95.
Prices include postage and handling. This offer is available in all countries.

Mail or fax Photocopy and complete the coupon below and post to ACP Books Reader Offer, ACP Publishing, GPO Box 4967, Sydney NSW 2001, or fax to (02) 9267 4967.

Phone Have your credit card details ready, then phone 136 116 (Mon-Fri, 8.00am-6.00pm; Sat, 8.00am-6.00pm).

Australian residents We accept the credit cards listed on the coupon, money orders and cheques.

Overseas residents We accept the credit cards listed on the coupon, drafts in $A drawn on an Australian bank, and also British, New Zealand and U.S. cheques in the currency of the country of issue. Credit card charges are at the exchange rate current at the time of payment.

Food director Pamela Clark
Food editor Louise Patniotis
ACP BOOKS STAFF
Editorial director Susan Tomnay
Creative director Hieu Nguyen
Senior editor Julie Collard
Designer Mary Keep
Publishing manager (sales) Jennifer McDonald
Publishing manager (rights & new titles) Jane Hazell
Assistant brand manager Donna Gianniotis
Pre-press by Harry Palmer
Production manager Carol Currie
Publisher Sue Wannan
Group publisher Jill Baker
Chief executive officer John Alexander
Produced by ACP Books, Sydney.
Printing by Dai Nippon Printing in Hong Kong.
Published by ACP Publishing Pty Limited, 54 Park St, Sydney; GPO Box 4088, Sydney, NSW 1028.
Ph: (02) 9282 8618 Fax: (02) 9267 9438.
acpbooks@acp.com.au
www.acpbooks.com.au
To order books phone 136 116.
Send recipe enquiries to Recipeenquiries@acp.com.au
Australia Distributed by Network Services, GPO Box 4088, Sydney, NSW 1028.
Ph: (02) 9282 8777 Fax: (02) 9264 3278.
United Kingdom Distributed by Australian Consolidated Press (UK), Moulton Park Business Centre, Red House Road, Moulton Park, Northampton, NN3 6AQ.
Ph: (01604) 497 531 Fax: (01604) 497 533.
acpukltd@aol.com
Canada Distributed by Whitecap Books Ltd, 351 Lynn Ave, North Vancouver, BC, V7J 2C4, Ph: (604) 980 9852.
New Zealand Distributed by Netlink Distribution Company, Level 4, 23 Hargreaves St, College Hill, Auckland 1, Ph: (9) 302 7616.

Clark, Pamela.
Wok.

Includes index.
ISBN 1 86396 278 6

1. Wok cookery.
I. Title. II. Title: Australian Women's Weekly (Series: Australian Women's Weekly mini series)
641.589

© ACP Publishing Pty Limited 2002
ABN 18 053 273 546
Cover: Lamb and cashew stir-fry, page 4.
Stylist: Sarah O'Brien
Photographer: Ian Wallace
Home economist for photography: Cathie Lonnie
Back cover: Sang choy bow (at left), page 49; Stir-fried seafood with Asian greens (at right), page 27.

Photocopy and complete coupon below

- ☐ **Book Holder** ☐ **Metric Measuring Set**
Please indicate number(s) required.

Mr/Mrs/Ms _____

Address _____

_____

Postcode _____ Country _____

Ph: Business hours ( ) _____

I enclose my cheque/money order for $ _____ payable to ACP Publishing.

OR: please charge $ _____ to my ☐ Bankcard ☐ Mastercard

☐ Visa ☐ American Express ☐ Diners Club

Expiry date ____ /____

| | | | | | | | | | | | | | | | | |

Card number

Cardholder's signature _____

Please allow up to 30 days delivery within Australia.
Allow up to 6 weeks for overseas deliveries.
Both offers expire 31/12/03. HLMW02